THE PILGRIMS' VOYAGE TO AMERICA

A FLY on the WALL HISTORY

BY THOMAS KINGSLEY TROUPE   ILLUSTRATED BY JOMIKE TEJIDO

PICTURE WINDOW BOOKS
a capstone imprint

Hi, I'm Horace, and this is my sister, Maggie.

We've been "flies on the wall" during important events in history.

We watched ancient Egyptians build the pyramids.

We saw Thomas Edison invent the lightbulb.

We even saw Jackie Robinson play his first major-league baseball game.

But when we were stowaways on the Mayflower? Now that was one stomach-turning trip ...

Maggie and I were buzzing around Southampton, England, in 1620. A group of people there didn't like their country's religion. As a result, they weren't treated very nicely. Some of them decided to leave and seek a fresh start in the New World. (That's what people in Europe called America back then.) They planned a voyage aboard two ships: the *Speedwell* and the *Mayflower*.

Why couldn't they start a new church in England? Or somewhere closer?

A few of them tried that in Holland.

Things didn't work out there either.

✸ ✸ ✸

Members of the Church of England were called Protestants. Some Protestants disagreed with the ways in which the Church was run. They were called Puritans. Some Puritans wanted to fix the Church. Those who didn't think it could be fixed were called Separatists (later called Pilgrims). They wanted to leave the Church completely.

✸ ✸ ✸

Maggie and I flew aboard the *Speedwell*. Great name for a ship, right? Well, maybe not. After seven days the *Speedwell* started to leak. Both ships stopped in Dartmouth, England, for repairs. A little over a week later, they set sail a second time.

But before long, the *Speedwell* was leaking again. The passengers and crewmembers tried to plug leaks and scoop up water. It didn't matter. The *Speedwell* had to go back to England. The *Mayflower* went back too.

Poor *Speedwell*.

Good thing it didn't start leaking in the middle of the ocean.

We could've flown back to shore. But the passengers sure would've had a long swim!

No kidding.

Maybe they should've named it *Leaks-well*!

The *Speedwell* couldn't be fixed. The *Mayflower* had to go to the New World alone. But not everyone could fit in one ship. The passengers had to figure out who would go and who would stay in England. It was a tough choice.

Maggie and I watched the passengers and sailors bring food and supplies on board. They even loaded dogs, cats, goats, pigs, and chickens.

Look at all the people and animals getting on the Mayflower.

It's going to be crowded!

And the people left behind seem pretty sad.

There just isn't enough room for everyone.

★ ★ ★

The *Mayflower* had 102 Puritans and 26 crewmembers when it left Plymouth, England. About half of the Puritans were Separatists (or Pilgrims). They called the non-Separatists on board "Strangers."

★ ★ ★

A man named Christopher Jones was the captain of the ship. Everyone called him Master Jones. He ordered young sailors to climb the masts and set the sails. Some of the bigger guys hauled up the anchor. That thing was really heavy!

Did you see where Master Jones stays?

He's got a great room on the upper deck.

It looks like all the sailors live up top.

Where is everyone else going to sleep?

★ ★ ★

The captain's living space is known as his quarters. It sits at the back of the ship. The captain's quarters is the most comfortable and driest area on board.

★ ★ ★

The lucky passengers on board waved goodbye to their friends staying behind. They knew they probably would never see them again.

Maggie and I checked out where the passengers were staying. It was pretty bad. They lived in a tight space called the lower deck. They shared it with the animals. Water regularly dripped through the ceiling. And the stink! I loved it, of course, but none of the passengers did. They couldn't bathe. They had to go to the bathroom—in buckets—with everyone else nearby. Many people got seasick and threw up.

I really don't feel well.
I wish I'd stayed back in England!

Here, use a bucket, Maggie.
Ooh ... maybe not this one.

No one wanted to risk setting the *Mayflower* on fire. So passengers ate food that didn't need to be cooked. They ate mostly hard biscuits, salted fish, moldy cheese, and dried beans and peas. Some of the food had bugs in it. (I met a weevil named Scott who loved eating the biscuits.)

* * *

The *Mayflower* was built to haul goods and supplies, not people. The lower deck was only 5.5 feet (1.7 meters) tall, 80 feet (24 m) long, and 14 feet (4.3 m) wide.

* * *

Life below deck was the worst! Maggie and I buzzed to the upper deck with some of the passengers. We needed to get some fresh air. Most of the *Mayflower*'s crewmembers didn't like that.

"Stay below deck!" they shouted.

One of the sailors was really mean. He yelled and made fun of the sick passengers. "I hope you die before our journey's end," he cried. "I'll be glad to be rid of you!"

He made it very clear that the passengers weren't welcome.

Wow! How rude!

That sailor really doesn't like having passengers aboard.

A bad living space, bad food, super-mean sailors ... what's next?

Maybe he thinks everyone will get in the way.

Still, that's no way to treat people.

As if things weren't bad enough, we ran into storms. Maggie and I watched the sailors try to keep the ship on course. Rain soaked the deck. Wind whipped the sails. Giant waves smashed into the Mayflower.

The Mayflower is really getting beat up. There's water everywhere!

No kidding! This boat ride hasn't been any fun.

Are we there yet?

Crewmembers worked quickly to lower the sails. The storms were so bad, Master Jones was afraid the wind would tear the sails loose. The ship was pretty helpless. We had to go wherever the weather took us. I just hoped we were still headed for the New World.

* * *

During some of the storms, the *Mayflower* had to face into the wind, to keep it from moving. To position the ship this way was to "heave to." Some storms forced the *Mayflower* to heave to for many days.

* * *

Back below deck the passengers grew more scared, wet, and miserable.
We'd been sailing for weeks by that time. We had faced lots of storms.
One of the men pointed to the main beam in the ceiling. It was cracked.

"The ship is coming apart!" he cried.

A few passengers hurried above deck to let the sailors know. Crewmembers got a new beam to replace the old one. But it needed to be held in place somehow. That's when one of the passengers offered up a huge screw. Together the sailors and passengers were able to fix the beam.

It's a good thing they had that screw, isn't it, Horace?

Yay for teamwork!

Who knows what would've happened without it?

Some historians believe the screw came from a printing press. It might have also been a house-building tool.

After the beam was fixed, the
Mayflower ran into more trouble.
During one of the storms, a man
named John Howland was washed
overboard. I thought he was done
for. But Maggie saw him grab
one of the ropes that hung
into the water.

Howland held on for dear life.
The crew tried to pull him up.
They even used a boat hook. They
struggled for a long time, but in
the end, they got Howland back
on the ship in one piece.

I don't think anywhere
on this ship is safe,
Horace.

I agree!
I like ships, but you know,
maybe England wasn't so
bad after all!

Life on the *Mayflower* was getting worse. Nothing was dry anymore. The lower deck smelled horrible. Lots of passengers got sick. A man named William Butten even died. He was wrapped in a sheet and buried at sea.

Some crewmembers got sick too. Remember that super-mean sailor I told you about? He got terribly sick and died. Some of the passengers believed God punished him for being mean.

* * *

Scurvy was a common disease among sailors. It's caused by lack of vitamin C.
People with scurvy usually have swollen, rotting gums. Their teeth often fall out.

* * *

It's sad knowing some of these folks won't ever make it to the New World.

Yes, it is.

But a new start is important to these passengers.

They'll risk everything for it ... even their lives!

Things weren't all bad on the *Mayflower*. One day something very special happened. A woman named Elizabeth Hopkins gave birth to a baby boy. (I admit I got a little teary-eyed.)

Elizabeth named the little guy Oceanus. Maggie and I thought it was a catchy name. I mean, what else would you name a baby born on the ocean? The other passengers helped make the new mom and baby as comfortable as possible.

I love that Lil' O's parents named him that. They named him after an important event in their lives.

Yep. The Mayflower's voyage is one event they'll never forget!

* * *

There were three pregnant women on the *Mayflower*. Oceanus Hopkins was the only baby born while sailing across the Atlantic Ocean.

* * *

In early November, Master Jones ordered a few sailors to climb the masts. He needed them to watch for land. I'm scared of heights, but Maggie isn't. She flew up the masts to see too.

After what seemed like forever, one of the sailors cried out.
He spotted land! Master Jones studied the charts. The *Mayflower*
was heading toward the tip of Cape Cod, in Massachusetts. We were
supposed to land much farther south. Our target was the mouth of
the Hudson River, in present-day New York. But it didn't matter.
We could see the New World!

How did the *Mayflower*
get so off course?

I blame the storms.

All the wind and rain
made it really tough
for Master Jones
and the crew.

I can't fly that well in
the rain either!

The *Mayflower* ended up 200 miles
(322 km) northeast of its
original target.

The New World!
Isn't this exciting,
Horace?

It almost makes
me forget
throwing up on
the ship.

It is! The trip over here
was really tough.

But I bet starting
a new life here is going
to be even tougher.

Master Jones ordered a few crewmembers to drop anchor. A few others went to the lower deck. They collected a bunch of wooden pieces and brought them up to the main deck. There they put them together and made a small boat called a shallop.

A group of passengers used the shallop to explore the coast. They were looking for the best place to start building their new homes.

* * *

It took 66 days to complete the 2,750-mile (4,426-km) journey to Cape Cod, Massachusetts.

* * *

The passengers in the shallop found a good place to settle along Plymouth Harbor. The *Mayflower* soon joined them. During the day, the Pilgrims built their new homes. In the evenings, they slept on the *Mayflower*.

Two people died during the journey to the New World, but more than half of the passengers died once there. The winter was cold and harsh. Many people died of starvation and disease. They didn't know how to grow crops in the new land. After some time, they met a Native American named Squanto. He showed them how to hunt and grow food. In the fall of 1621, the Pilgrims and members of Squanto's tribe shared a harvest feast.

TIMELINE

1607
The English settle in Jamestown, Virginia.

AUGUST 1620
The *Mayflower* and the *Speedwell* set sail for the New World. Only the *Mayflower* is able to continue the voyage.

DECEMBER 16, 1620
The *Mayflower* arrives in Plymouth Harbor.

1621
Forty-five of the 102 passengers on the *Mayflower* die of disease and starvation in the first winter. They are buried on Cole's Hill.

MARCH 1621
The Pilgrims have their first contact with Native Americans.

APRIL 1621
The *Mayflower* and its crewmembers return to England.

JULY 1621
Native Americans teach the Pilgrims how to farm, hunt, and fish.

OCTOBER 1621
The Pilgrims and Native Americans celebrate the harvest together.

1630
John Winthrop leads a large number of Puritans from England to settle in the New World. He becomes the governor of the Massachusetts Bay Colony, the largest settlement in New England after Plymouth.

GLOSSARY

anchor–a heavy metal hook that is lowered from a ship to keep it from drifting

colony–an area that has been settled by people from another country; a colony is ruled by another country

harvest–to gather crops that are ready to eat

mast–a tall pole on a ship's deck that holds its sails

Pilgrim–another name for a Separatist

Puritan–a dissatisfied member of the Church of England; most Puritans wanted to fix the Church from within; many settled in the Massachusetts Bay Colony

Separatist–an extremely dissatisfied Puritan who wanted to start a new church; Separatists settled in Plymouth Colony; also called a Pilgrim

shallop–a small open boat outfitted with oars or sails

starvation–suffering or dying from lack of food

voyage–a long journey

THINK ABOUT IT

1. The Pilgrims had a very long and rough ride across the ocean to reach the New World. Describe some of the hardships they endured along the way. (Key Ideas and Details)

2. Some of the sailors on the *Mayflower* were mean to the passengers. Why do you think they treated the passengers so poorly? (Integration of Knowledge and Ideas)

3. Even though the voyage was harsh, more Pilgrims died in the New World than on the ship. Why? (Integration of Knowledge and Ideas)

READ MORE

Cook, Peter. *You Wouldn't Want to Sail on the Mayflower! : A Trip That Took Entirely Too Long.* You Wouldn't Want To. New York: Franklin Watts, an imprint of Scholastic Inc., 2014.

deRubertis, Barbara. *Let's Celebrate Thanksgiving Day.* Holidays and Heroes. New York: The Kane Press, 2013.

Troupe, Thomas Kingsley. *Your Life as a Settler in Colonial America.* The Way It Was. North Mankato, Minn.: Picture Window Books, 2012.

INTERNET SITES

FactHound offers a safe, fun way to find Internet sites related to this book.
All of the sites on FactHound have been researched by our staff.

Here's all you do:
Visit *www.facthound.com*
Type in this code: 9781479597864

Check out projects, games and lots more at
www.capstonekids.com

Super-cool stuff!

INDEX

birth, 22–23

Butten, William, 20

Cape Cod, Massachusetts, 25, 27

cracked beam, 16–18

crewmembers, 5, 6, 7, 8, 12–15, 17, 18, 20, 24–25, 27, 29

death, 13, 20, 28, 29

disease, 20, 28, 29

England, 3, 4, 5, 6, 7, 10, 18, 29

food, 6, 11, 13, 28, 29

Hopkins, Elizabeth, 22–23

Hopkins, Oceanus, 22–23

Howland, John, 18

Jones, Christopher, 8, 24–25, 27

leaks, 4–5

length of voyage, 27

lower deck, 10–11, 16–17, 20, 27

Native Americans, 28, 29

New World, 3, 6, 21, 25, 26, 28, 29

Pilgrims. *See* Separatists

Plymouth Harbor, 28, 29

Protestants, 3

Puritans, 3, 7, 29

sailors. *See* crewmembers

seasickness, 10, 13, 20

Separatists, 3, 7, 28, 29

Speedwell, 3–6, 29

storms, 14–16, 18, 25

upper deck, 8, 12

Winthrop, John, 29

Look for all the books in the series:

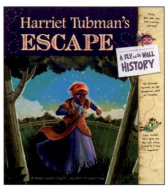
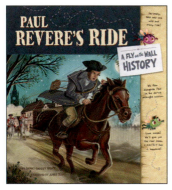

Special thanks to our adviser, Kevin Byrne, PhD, Professor Emeritus of History, Gustavus Adolphus College, for his expertise.

Picture Window Books is published by Capstone,
1710 Roe Crest Drive, North Mankato, Minnesota 56003
www.mycapstone.com

Library of Congress Cataloging-in-Publication Data
Names: Troupe, Thomas Kingsley, author.
Title: The Pilgrims' voyage to America : a Fly on the wall history / by Thomas Kingsley Troupe.
Description: North Mankato, Minnesota : Picture Window Books, an imprint of Capstone Press, [2017] | Series: Nonfiction picture books. Fly on the wall history | Audience: K to grade 3. | Includes bibliographical references and index.
Identifiers: LCCN 2016034401 | ISBN 9781479597864 (library binding) | ISBN 9781479597901 (paperback) | ISBN 9781479597949 (PDF)
Subjects: LCSH: Pilgrims (New Plymouth Colony)–Juvenile literature. | Mayflower (Ship)–Juvenile literature. | Ocean travel–History–17th century–Juvenile literature. | Massachusetts–History–New Plymouth, 1620-1691–Juvenile literature.
Classification: LCC F68 .T76 2017 | DDC 974.4/02–dc23
LC record available at https://lccn.loc.gov/2016034401

Editor: Jill Kalz
Designer: Sarah Bennett
Creative Director: Nathan Gassman
Production Specialist: Steve Walker

The illustrations in this book were planned with pencil on paper and finished with digital paints.

Printed and bound in the USA
010059S17CG